BURN out, don't RUST

BURN out, don't RUST

THE LIFE of JOHN PUGH

Phil Rees

Contents

Acknowledgements

My thanks are due to a number of friends who have helped:

To Professor Denzil Morgan for hours of kind advice;

To my friend Dr Gwendraith Morgan, for translations from the Welsh language;

To Noel Gibbard, and Roger Brown, for help with the historical background;

To Professor John Gallagher, for help with the text and for his wise suggestions;

And to my Editor, Joe Laycock, for so much willing work.

Above all, thanks to Kate, my wife, for her encouragement, corrections and typing.

Foreword

by Roger Forster

I have heard it said Wales experienced as many as ten revivals of faith in the nineteenth century. These were contributory preludes to the great Welsh revival of 1904. I have no documented evidence that there were precisely ten, however, Phil Rees' account of John Pugh's life and work of evangelism and church planting demonstrates that Wales in the 1800s was particularly blessed with outpourings of Christian life and spirituality through many men and women of renown like John Pugh, as well as many unsung and unremembered heroes. The ensuing revival of 1904 impacted the whole world church and contributed to the preservation of vital Christianity through two horrifying world wars. Our debt to Welsh Christianity is immense and so by implication is our debt to John Pugh among others. We are indebted also to Phil Rees for reviving John's story for us today.

As we read we will grow in appreciation of this man of God and learn essential qualities for our own service for Christ. The necessary elements in Christian workers are, and always have been, the same. Now, over 100 years after John Pugh proclaimed Jesus as Lord, we too need hard work, persistence, prayer and preaching in the streets, all of which we will find in him. As I write I have just returned from a Saturday doing cold-contact evangelism in the streets, a Sunday rallying and preaching in the open air and 'marching for Jesus'. The world must see we are here. Eye to eye contact, in our day of technology and virtual realities, is essential for spiritual breakthrough even as much as in John Pugh's day where open air preaching is fundamental to his success.

Revival is basically God sending His Spirit in Jesus' name. At Pentecost the fire came on the disciples and burned until they burnt out at death, not in nervous breakdown. John Pugh wanted that burning life of love for Jesus Christ. Phil's alternative is in the title of his book *Burn Out, Don't Rust*. Rusting is the result of the Spirit (like rain cf. Joel 2:23–28) being poured out but our never responding to move with Him in obedience, or having begun, never to continue. Perseverance will keep us from rusting as it kept John Pugh. It is a mark of an Apostle (2 Corinthians 12:12) according to Paul.

'Lord send your Spirit in Jesus' Name.' This Prayer of Evan Roberts of the Welsh Revival is for all who are reading this book, so well-constructed and challenging, from Phil Rees' pen. This is my prayer for you and of course myself as also is this longing for the church in the West.

> Therefore, my beloved brothers, be steadfast, immovable, always abounding in the work of the Lord, knowing that your toil is not in vain in the Lord.
> (1 Corinthians 15:58)

Paul's prayer for us and John Pugh's example are Phil's legacy to all his readers.

R.T. Forster
March 2016

Introduction

I have wanted to write this story for more than thirty years, since I first read about the work of John Pugh. For most of my Christian life I had learned about the Great Awakening in the Eighteenth Century, and I had loved and valued especially the days and work of Daniel Rowland. I also learned of what happened in 1904 and the years following, which included the birth of Pentecostal Churches and a great missionary movement which went out into so many lands, especially in what we call the Far East. I have recently met numerous Korean Christians who all said the same things. They have come to Wales to say 'Thank you' to us for our part in evangelising their nation. They look back with thanksgiving to what happened in Wales in 1904 and the following years, as it changed their nation.

I knew that in the nineteenth century there were significant moves of the Holy Spirit in our world, and in our islands, but until I met with John Pugh, I did not see how the Lord prepared the people of Wales for 1904 and what followed. He was not the only one, of course.

Elsewhere in the book, I will mention some of the many servants who were involved in revival in the years before 1904. The Lord was digging deeply into the nation in so many places, where some spoke Welsh, and others English.

But I felt so close to John Pugh. It would be arrogant to say he is a man after my own heart, but I would wish to be a man after his heart. There is so much in John that I love, so I wanted to tell this story.

Phil Rees
2016

1

Birth to Second Birth

John Pugh was born in New Mills, Montgomery in 1846. His parents, John senior, and Ann, were loving and devout. Ann's father was a splendid old man who was called Rowland, and he had a gift for opening and explaining the Scriptures to others. Ann's Uncle John, brother to Rowland, was a self-taught student who mastered English, and gained knowledge of Latin, Greek and Hebrew. He was widely recognised as a leader of his denomination. He spoke powerfully, wrote widely on Christian themes, and wrote and collected hymns in the Welsh language.

The family were Calvinistic Methodists and it was in that tradition that the baby, John, was to be raised. It was a secure home in which Welsh was the first language. John was influenced by the border country in which he grew up, and was soon proficient in English also. From childhood he was a tender-hearted and kind personality. We can be sure his mother's influence and prayer for her son was very significant. New Mills Church was in the vigour and enthusiasm of its early days. John became a member before he was fourteen, and he then held open-air meetings amongst his neighbours. In 1860, at the height of a great move of the Holy Spirit in the USA, Britain and Europe, the family moved to

Tenby in Pembrokeshire. John's father was a contractor, who had been used in the building of bridges.

That was the early part of a railway building boom, and John senior had worked for David Davies of Llandinam, who became perhaps the greatest industrialist of the nineteenth century in Wales. The family was now in Tenby, so that John Pugh senior could build bridges on the Pembroke and Tenby Railway for David Davies. John junior was taken on by the managers as an assistant to his father, and must have learned a deal about building. This would help in his future life. As a young clerk, John was seen as 'something of a dandy'! He was always sociable and generous, and liked the company of other people, especially those of his own age, on the streets or in the public houses. At the same time, he was regularly found in his place at Sunday services at Begelly Chapel, and in the Sunday school. There must have been some tension in him at this time, for he was very aware of the pull of the world's attractions. The good inheritance of his home and family was, in the end, not overthrown. After 'sitting on the fence' for some time, John was being prepared by the Holy Spirit for his conversion, and his personal call to serve the Lord Jesus. Those who knew him well were able to identify three elements in this preparation. Of course, there were others, of which we know nothing.

First, there was a promise he had made to an aunt that he would read some part of the Bible every day. He sought to keep that promise, and we can imagine that the Holy Spirit worked in those times, as John tried to understand what he was reading. This was strengthened by the situation in the chapel with the teaching and leadership of his friends.

There came a second influence, in a moment when he was unwell. Unable to attend the service or Sunday school, he picked up and read part of a magazine left by his mother in his room.

Christian mothers do such things. It was in October 1866, in an edition of *Y Drysorfa* and he read an article by Rev. William Charles, written when the author was only twenty-three. This hit John hard, and disturbed his thinking and the satisfaction he felt with his current life. The message was based on Revelation 1 verse 17,

> When I saw Him, I fell at His feet like a dead man.
> And He placed His right hand on me, saying, "Do
> not be afraid; I am the First and the Last."

John never forgot that great truth. It impacted him that day, and was with him for the rest of his life on this earth.

The third was a challenge from new friends. Before the end of the year, John, now aged twenty, was to take the step of faith which brought him to be a disciple of the Lord Jesus, and an inheritor of the Kingdom of Heaven. Two students played the major part in this big challenge which was to change his life. Thomas Charles Edwards came to Tenby during vacations between 1863 and 1869. Under the benevolent provision of David Davies, he and others were to bring the Gospel to the railway workers, the navigators or 'Navvies', who were making the railway line. A simple building was provided as a meeting place for the men, and for teaching and worship to take place. Thomas Charles Edwards later became the first Principal of the University College at Aberystwyth, and then moved to be Principal of the Ministerial Training College at Bala. Listening to Edwards, and another student, David Lloyd Jones, John came to know that he was not really a Christian. There came the moment when he made his decision to step forward and follow the Lord Jesus. Behind this decision, which millions of men women and children have made, and which is termed 'conversion', 'being saved', or in Jesus' own words to Nicodemus, being 'Born of the Spirit', or 'Born Again', lies the truly Christian view of the world and humanity.

Heavenly Father has decreed with the Son and the Holy Spirit that the answer to man's fallen state in the world in every generation, is the provision of the Son, Jesus. He does a great work for us all, and offers us an invitation to benefit, in the way planned, from that work. Humanity, already born in the flesh, must be re-born in the Holy Spirit, who shows Jesus. There is no other way. A man may choose to stay in his natural fallen state, or he may surrender to the provision made for him by Jesus, and revealed to him by the Holy Spirit.

The young builder, John Pugh, grasped this salvation and began a new life in the Holy Spirit. The natural gifting which John had always demonstrated, prepared him for his future call and ministry. He had always cared for people. He had a kind compassionate and loving nature. Now he longed to share his own joy and security with all. He did not know of any means of devoting his life to evangelism except by following the path of training for ministry in the denomination.

2

Preparation

Both David Lloyd Jones and Thomas Charles Edwards were to become his life-long friends, and always afterwards John explained how his response to Jesus involved their initiative, prayer and help.

As a young new Christian, John had not only a supportive family but also a true friend in his minister, Revd. George Bancroft, the Pastor of the Begelly Presbyterian Church. He provided books and periodicals, and was eager to help John in many ways. During these weeks John became aware that on becoming a new creation he had received from the Holy Spirit a new depth of love for others and a passion regarding their lostness whilst they were without the Lord.

It was not love for humanity in the mass, but a very personal care for individual men, women and children that he knew or met.

He loved to sing a chorus which ran: 'If Jesus found you, tell others the story . . .' He began to fill his life with 'telling'. He gathered other young people around him and held open air meetings where he might share his experience. This ministry was sourced in prayer and in the guidance of the Holy Spirit. It deepened his spiritual life.

When first converted he had no intention of becoming a full-time church minister of the Gospel. More than any plan for his future in a calling or profession, he began to know that open-air work in the midst of the workday scene was to be the first principle of any plan of campaign. In fact, his time as a secular builder was coming to an end. He was encouraged, step by step, by the Revd. Barcroft, and by other mature Christian ministers, to seek a future as one of them.

He did discover the call of the Lord on his life to go that way, but he always carried with him the enthusiasm of being 'God's man', and the determination to reach the lost. He could not look forward to the 'comfortable' preaching and pastoral ministry in a well established congregation. He would always be seeking lost souls, pressing out with the help of the Holy Spirit, into the rapidly changing world of industrial South Wales, where most of the growing population was to be found. It would mean ministry by word and deed in his second language, English, to people who knew very little of the Bible, the work of Jesus or the Church.

From the 1730s, until John's day, the expectation of evangelists in Wales was 'revival power'. The history of Wales, from the time of Howell Harris and Daniel Rowland, was marked by many outbreaks of this experience in congregations, towns and regions. A host of gospel ministers were involved, in the Welsh language, and the expectation of an evangelical like John, was that if the good news of the Lord Jesus was faithfully spoken to the people, then the work of the Holy Spirit would bring individuals and situations to revival. John's early years were in a period which experienced the out-pouring of 1858–1863, which so influenced the States of North America and all the nations of the British Isles. In all he wished to do, John realised he could not rely on the ideas of men in beginning the work, but put himself firmly under the influence of the Holy Spirit. His prayer was that He would come powerfully, bringing revival depths and significance. John had the great comfort of being completely 'at home' with people on the streets and in the places of industry. In the late nineteenth century people spent most of their lives at work or on the streets. The road ways of valley towns and villages were thronged with men, women and children.

John sought to be prepared for his life of service at the denominational college at Trevecca. He passed the entrance examinations, and in the autumn term of 1869 he began his formal studies. He was twenty-three years of age, and his Principal was William Howells. He was to study from 'books' for three years, but his daughter tells us that,

> The thrill of the Gospel had taken hold of him, and the call of 'Souls' was in his ears.

He was more than adequate in his academic work, but it soon became evident that he stood out amongst his fellow students as an evangelist.

John Hughes was a student at Trevecca at the same time and he speaks very warmly of John Pugh,

> He was the most distinguished of students for personality and presence, with a ready and graceful address which stood us in good stead whenever visitors obtruded into the solitude of our studies.

He adds, looking back over many years,

> He was raised to be the great evangelist of our church, nor do I think that a greater one was given to any church.

The Principal set aside several Saturday mornings each term for the subject of the principles and practices of preaching. Part of the time was spent listening to one of the students presenting a message to his fellows as if before a congregation. At the end of the address, the other students were asked for their comments and after a particular student addressed them, eventually it came to John's turn to comment. 'Well', he said,

> I agree with much that is said in favour of the sermon we have heard. The diction was polished and the periods well rounded and all that; but I hope our brother is not going to preach that sermon to any congregation, for it has one fatal defect – it will never save a single soul.

For John, this is always the heart of the matter. In all Christian communication, the vital ingredients are to make folk aware of their need of a Saviour, and then to show that the Lord Jesus is the only answer. Although John's classical and theological training was, of necessity, brief, he never belittled education, provided that it served the great end of pointing to Father's love shown in the Gospel. For the work to which he had been called, he was anointed by the Holy Spirit, his natural gifts were employed, and he built upon the knowledge of the Word he had acquired since infancy. He knew he was to be a workman who learned rightly to handle the tools that the Lord had provided. He welcomed any learned ministry provided that it was visited by the presence of the Holy Spirit. Though eager to be 'let loose' for his life's work, he made full use of his college days. He cultivated friendships which remained alive and real ever afterwards. He had a mixture of mature gifts together with the burning desire to speak out to a fallen world. His support, kindness, loyalty and generosity, with a sense of fun, were the marks of his life, even at the age of twenty-nine. He longed to set out on that life-long missionary journey. He blessed those at Trevecca, but his call was to be to the teeming thousands of industrial Wales in their extreme spiritual need.

3

Great Days at Tredegar

The Lord was already preparing the specific venue for John's first vital attack on the powers of darkness. From the same area of rural Wales in Pembrokeshire, in the years 1869–1872, many young men travelled to the industrial areas to find work and 'better' themselves. Some arrived at the works and coal mines of Tredegar and the Sirhowy Valley. Four Christian brothers named Badham, previously members of Seion Begelly Calvinistic Methodist Church, and who knew John well, migrated there, and they were, with others, founders of a Christian meeting place, the 'Tin Chapel'. John's spiritual journey, and his desire to influence his former friends for Jesus, had blessed them. The chapel was on the 'Cinder Tip', now called Vale Terrace. The building was small and ugly and the members numbered less than twenty, but they possessed faith and some vision. They decided they needed a man to lead and teach them, and so they sought a 'Minister'. They remembered how John's conversion had transformed him, and how he had held meetings in the churches around Tenby.

The same eagerness to go to work amongst his former friends, which gripped John Pugh, was also to be felt in the small gathering of the chapel. They thought that the Lord's choice was John, and when he knew of it, he felt a strong desire to respond. He had received other calls. His daughter writes,

> He curtailed his college course by a year so as to be able to go out to the work, and his request was granted, thus instigating the beginning of a powerful ministry of wondrous influence which continues to this day.

The friendship between the young man who had come, and his former friends, who had been guided to call him, deepened and strengthened. He was their friend as well as their leader. They worshipped and played together; in that mining area the favourite outdoor game was quoits, and on a summer's evening at the back of Georgetown terraces in Tredegar, John and his friends enjoyed many a game. He was a handsome young man, strong, with a sympathetic face, and a thickness of flowing beard. He also possessed a tuneful voice which carried well. He began his work there on the first Sunday of July in 1872, supported by the Home Missions Board of the denomination, with £25 per annum. The small congregation agreed to add another £25 from their own sacrificial giving, a real venture of faith. The cause had now been in existence for about five years, beginning in a rough builders shanty for the purpose of studying the Bible together. Eight regulars had moved to the Tin Chapel. In the first weeks in Tredegar, despite appearances, John knew that he was in the place of the Lord's choosing. He expected blessings to follow in this town; his longing from the start was for the many men, women and children who knew nothing of the Lord Jesus and Father's love. There were crowds in the streets to be reached. No-one seemed to be seeking them with the Gospel. The church life was mostly in the Welsh language, and yet few of the many he saw on the streets were able to read or speak in Welsh.

From the beginning John was sharing his vision of outreach with the deacons of his little fellowship. They did not oppose him, but some did not seem to share his enthusiasm. He proposed his first move on the last Sunday of that July. It was advertised that on the Tuesday evening, at seven o'clock, an open-air service would be held at 'the Clock'. This was the centre of 'the Circle', a significant focal point in the town.

What John began that evening was to save many in his denomination and other churches from a 'maintenance' mentality. It was a time when the passion of earlier generations was settling into respectability. Seven o'clock was passed and John stood alone in the passing crowds. Then six women from his fellowship came to join him. He told them he would sing a hymn and asked them to join him in the chorus, 'I am coming Lord, Coming now to Thee'. Then, eyes closed, he prayed for the presence and help of the Lord. He said,

> When I opened my eyes, after being on the mount with God, a crowd of men and women stood before me gazing in amazement into my eyes.

At the sound of singing, some who stood around were challenged at the effrontery of a minister intruding on their territory. John knew how to approach working men, for he had work experience with the railway navvies, and in the pubs before that. He began,

> Boys, they tell me that you are an awful set here, and that you were in the habit of throwing rotten eggs and mud at a dear old minister, who used to stand up here and tell you of Jesus and His love. I am not afraid of anyone in this crowd, but I am awfully afraid of myself, for if any of you should insult me and I lose my temper, I should surely mark that man.

A local collier took John's side, and demanded that he be given a fair hearing.

> Go on youngster; I'll stand by you. The man who insults you will have to reckon with me.

Soon the meetings at the Clock became a regular fixture.

Crowds gathered to listen, and this was reflected in the attendance at the Tin Chapel. Commentators have said that here began what later became the 'Forward Movement' – a concerted aggressive evangelism all over South Wales, including church planting in many places. But that lay in the future. For now, there was opposition. It came not from the colliers or anti-Christian groups, but from some of the established Christian churches in the town. He was called a 'Ranter', a reference back to the 'Ranter's Revival' of the 1830s, a word which surely should have been a badge of honour. Some opposition came even from his own denomination.

The news of what was happening in Tredegar spread far and wide, and two honoured men visited the meeting on an evening at the Clock. They had been prompted to come because of the grumbling they heard in a chapel in which they were speaking. They were Revd. Edward Matthews and John's old Principal from Trevecca, William Howells. They stood in the crowd at the Clock as John spoke. The Holy Spirit moved, and people were touched in different ways, including some who wanted to respond to the invitation to follow Jesus. John recounts what happened next,

> Edward Matthews came up to me, and putting his two hands upon my shoulders, he closed his eyes and said 'God bless you, my boy. I am thankful that Howell Harris is not dead. I never felt myself such a big sinner as I am now, for had I and others done this in our life,

Glamorganshire and Monmouthshire would not be in
the grip of the evil one'.

John responded, that the deacons who had come with Mr
Matthews saw him as no Methodist, and a dragger of the Gospel
into the dirt. Edward Matthews replied, 'It is you who are the
true Methodist. This is Methodism' – meaning what they were
seeing at the Clock. 'This' he said, 'is what made Welsh Wales
what it is today, and this is what must transform Glamorganshire
and Monmouthshire.' From that night on, many critical elders
and deacons in the town became keen supporters. The fellowship
in the Tin Chapel continued to grow, with increased spiritual
life, conversions and signs of the activity of the work of the
Holy Spirit.

Many showed the grace of an evangelistic passion. Because of
the growth, the Temperance Hall, with seating for 1,000, was
hired for Sunday evenings. It became well filled, and usually
there were many young people. The open-air work at the Clock
continued, and the crowd grew so large that the townspeople
intervened and decided to erect strong iron rails around the clock
to protect it.

This was a blessing for the speaker, for now John had become
a favourite with the town authorities, and he was able to take a
prominent place within the railings with his helpers. Many were
deeply moved by the Holy Spirit at these gatherings. One hot
Sunday evening the pubs around were full, with their windows
open because of the heat. John shouted in his strong voice, 'It is
stop tap in hell', repeating the challenge over and over again. It
had such an effect on one man that he left his beer on the bar,
never to return again to the pub. In the week-night meetings
in a few days, he expressed a desire to join them. At a monthly
meeting, which regulated church affairs, the question arose as to

how the growing congregation, and the many outreach activities, with men, women and children, could be accommodated. John favoured flexibility, but it was agreed to construct a large building. So in the first four years at Tredegar a building, later known as Park Place was built, with the big population at Georgetown behind it. It was to seat 700 folk, and John's father was used as the builder. The small membership that had called John had now increased to over four hundred, and there was a Sunday school of four hundred and fifty. In later years he was to declare that the real birthplace of the Forward Movement was the circle around the clock in Tredegar.

The evangelist heart of John Pugh was not satisfied until his preaching bore fruit by changing the condition of the crowds, so that they moved in response, from death to life. As Jesus said with Zacchaeus, 'Salvation has come', and so it was for so many in Tredegar. The real humility of John meant that he knew it was all of the Lord, and he was so pleased that the Lord was willing to use him as an instrument of Heaven's Blessing.

4

Marriage and Widening Work

One of the churches in Monmouthshire that invited John to visit and preach at was 'Mozerah' near the rural market town of Abergavenny, which was about fifteen miles from Tredegar. There, in the congregation, John saw the girl to whom he was immediately attracted. As he began to know her, they realised that they shared the same passion for Jesus, and the same desire to see souls saved. She was Marie Watkins, the daughter of a successful farmer, John Watkins. He owned and lived at a farm called 'Pentre' near Raglan. Her mother's family had long been involved in the work at Mozerah, and one of her ancestors was a founder member there. When it became clear that Marie and John had an 'understanding', it was not news that was welcome with Marie's parents. No doubt they would have preferred a rich farmer for their daughter, and John's financial situation seemed poor. They foretold an unhappy future for Marie. If she married a minister with the Calvinistic Methodists, she would face a life of hard labour and utter obscurity. They did not dislike John Pugh, but they thought marriages were not made in heaven, rather in the world of land and money. Income deserved the greatest consideration.

In reply, John argued the promises of the Word of the Lord,

'The Book', which promised sufficient provision for those who first sought the Kingdom of God and placed their care on Him. So in due time, John and Marie were married in Abergavenny. Marie was not only at one with her husband in all spiritual matters, but she was able to fit herself for the ministry that lay ahead. Like John she was a strong character. She had personality and courage. This last gift was the one which she would really need and in which she excelled. She was influential, and her strength was tempered by great kindness and a warm heart. She loved Jesus and longed always to serve Him with her husband, John. Her compassion for the lost matched that of his. They stood together, the one partaking of the other's joy, and gave themselves unstintingly to the work of the Lord.

The ministry of John at Tredegar had become well known throughout Wales. There were pressing invitations to move to other places of worship in other towns. John knew the call to serve in Tredegar was not yet at an end. As each new opportunity was presented, he declined with a light heart. He knew the great secret for a minister – blessing flows when a person is in the place of the Lord's choice. When that place is known, it carries with it not only a strategy, but real vision for that time.

The work of the people of Tredegar was encountering one of those periodic economic slumps, which come to industries, and John was close to the lives of the working people. He felt deeply for them in their struggles and sought ways to help them in their distress. But things then improved once more and the church was now in a stable prosperous state. It continued to grow, and had not lost it's evangelistic thrust. John knew he could move on and leave behind a team of real evangelists. He was also anxious to 'pioneer' as an evangelist in another place where things seemed spiritually dead. He felt clearly guided, in total agreement with

Marie, that he should accept an invitation to come to St. David's Church in Pontypridd, about eighteen miles away. It was an old town in the Taff Valley, halfway between Merthyr Tydfil and Cardiff, which had been overwhelmed by the amazing growth of population in the area.

The coal mines of the Rhondda Valleys, to the north of Pontypridd, had really begun with the work of David Davies, about fifteen years earlier. People had flooded into the new area as the work developed. It was to be a much stiffer task than that which he had faced in Tredegar. John and Marie accepted this new move in the early months of 1881, and began the ministry there on the first Sunday in April. The town was generally believed to be very uncivilised. Many of the migrant workers, some with families, spoke no Welsh, which was the usual language of the tradespeople and the chapels. An English cause had been started in 1878, but it had no base of its own – it used the vestry of a Welsh church.

John found in his new pastorate a degree of complacency. The fellowship felt confident of its future, carrying on the work 'On the old stereotyped traditional Calvinistic lines', as Howell Williams tells us. It was the same old story as at Tredegar. There was a multitude of people, left out of all Christian care, with very feeble attempts made by the churches to bring it the good news of Jesus. As in all their lives, John and Marie had come to the region of Pontypridd to reach out to such a crowd, using whatever means they could. There was by the railway station a square which was called 'The Tumble'. There were found seventeen drinking shops or public houses. The local men were called 'The Tumble Gang' and it was so notorious a spot, that it was called 'Little hell'.

5

Breaking Through In Pontypridd

John Pugh saw The Tumble as the obvious place to begin an open-air campaign. On the last Sunday evening of April, in his first month in Pontypridd, he announced that on the Saturday evening following, at seven, he would hold an open-air meeting on The Tumble. He invited his congregation to meet him there. The officers of the fellowship gave him no opposition, but neither did they encourage him. He was there at seven o'clock on that Saturday evening, but no-one turned up to support him. He was not dismayed. He says in his 'Reminiscences':

> Before me, there was a gang of about two dozen powerful, rough looking men who were in deep consultation about a coming fight. I went up to them and said, 'Men, I propose preaching in this spot this evening, but I don't see any saints about here to stand by me, only some poor sinners like myself – for I once belonged to your school – but I have given up knocking men about. I have taken to fighting the devil and his imps. Will you stand by me, for I am a stranger here?' 'We don't mind Sir', was the reply. 'Thank you. Will you please form a ring?'

Then, stepping into the ring of men, John sang a solo. Then

he spoke, with humour and lots of illustrations. This unusual Christian approach held the crowd. At the close he invited his listeners to the service at the vestry on the next day. They came, a crowd of them, and filled up the room on the next evening. The open-air meetings became established at The Tumble on Saturday nights, and went from strength to strength. Vigorous opposition was stirred up, mainly from the getting together of the owners of the seventeen public houses. One Saturday evening a very drunken man was sent into the crowd near to where John was speaking. Another time a town crier was hired to ring a bell in the area to spoil the meeting. Finally they hired a brass band to perform at the same time that John stood up. John said, 'When they got puffed, I preached!'

In the midst of the tumult of the Saturday night pleasure fairs, including Punch and Judy shows, and quacks selling 'cures', as well as the brass band, John would take his stand, and he soon succeeded in gathering around him scores of people who would join him in the singing and listen as he opened the Scriptures. The effect was felt both in his own congregation, and also amongst those who never attended a place of worship.

The attempts to disrupt the open-air times did not work. They brought criticism down on the heads of those responsible, from many in the town. The controversy proved to be an excellent advert for what John was doing. Larger crowds grew as the opposition mounted.

The conflict with the drinking dens of Pontypridd led to a Temperance Mission in January 1882. Throughout his Christian life, John felt that the liquor trade was often the chief enemy to the sharing of the Gospel in the South Wales scene, dominated by the coal industry. He wanted to reach working men and break their dependence on drink and the places where drink was sold. Many turned to drink as an escape from a life of privation, hardship, overcrowding and lack of the basic amenities of life. In Tredegar John had begun a temperance movement. He had, in 1872, devoted himself to the Good Templars Movement, of which he became the first deputy from Monmouthshire, and he had the pleasure of seeing as many as 1,500 members in Tredegar. In Pontypridd there was no sign of a similar movement, so with some ardent friends, the campaign of the Army of the Blue Ribbon was begun in that January. It was led by John, W.J. Morris, and a good friend invited over from America, R.T. Booth. During the mission more than 2,000 people signed the pledge in one period of two weeks. Amongst them was one who was to become the leading light and chief evangelist of the future 'Forward Movement' – Seth Joshua signed the pledge in the January, and surrendered his life to Jesus in the April. The campaign through the month of January undermined the finances of scores of public houses in the Pontypridd district.

A journalist, writing in the Pontypridd Chronicle in 1882, under the assumed name of Awstin, gave a pen-picture of John. He wrote,

> His constant and consistent opposition to the liquor trade – for he was a friend of the public and not the publican – brought him into antagonism with the liquor traffickers, and even the magisterial bench which has the power to suppress or advance the greatest enemy of the law. This, on one occasion, almost landed him in Cardiff prison. He was not prepared to apologise to the Bench for the strong things he had uttered about their conduct; but he was quite prepared to go to prison, if it would save the people and open the eyes of the Bench on the evil of strong drink. But when the people saw

that he was in danger they rallied round him so that the Bench wisely allowed the matter to drop, and Mr Pugh lost a holiday in 'The Queen's Temperance Hotel' in Cardiff.

John triumphed in other conflicts in the town. He quickly became a spiritual force there, and, as in his ministry at Tredegar, he believed that the offer of salvation in Jesus to a needy people carried with it, for Christians, an impetus to social action and sometimes, political action. There was always a need for love in action.

Preaching in the open air became the norm in evangelistic outreach, and at the same time, the premises for the congregation were proved to be inadequate. The Sunday evening services were overfull, and so within two years a new chapel, named St David's, was erected. The congregation was growing into hundreds during this time, but the emphasis was always on reaching the unreached. Many buildings he was involved with were grand, but to John, they were only tools to be used, and not valuable in themselves. He would only take pride in what the Lord was doing in such places. His many contacts meant that he could invite notable missioners for numerous evangelistic missions. One visitor, now famous in Victorian Britain, was H.M. Stanley, who had searched for, and found, Dr Livingston in Africa. Once again we may quote the journalist 'Awstin' on the ministry of John Pugh to the crowds.

> Though speaking English in the pulpit, he is endowed with all the fire of his race, combined with the polished diction imparted by careful preparation for the pulpit; his fluency is increased by his earnestness; and his appeals cannot help being effective, for they evidently come from a heart burning with a desire to save souls, and a soul imbued with the faith that moves mountains.

Evangelistic speakers invited to Pontypridd also included a very good friend, Rev. William Ross of Cowcaddens Free Church of Scotland, in Glasgow. Ross had ministered lovingly and effectively to the poor people of that city, where alcohol was the major destroyer of lives, as in South Wales. What he shared with John was a great encouragement, and many ideas and methods of work were talked over between the two.

Apart from the drinking places, there were so few amenities in the town catering to the cultural needs of the people. John wanted to open the world to the people through good literature. He also wanted to help folk improve their level of education. He advocated a free library for the town. The licensed victuallers were opposed to the costs involved for rate payers, but more, they thought a library would be an attractive alternative to their monopoly on leisure time in the public houses. A poll of rate payers was organised on the question for or against a library. Mr R.J. Rowland, an elder of Plasnewydd Church, Cardiff, tells us what happened:

> When the polling day came, Mr L. Gordon Lennox, head of the Chain works, sat as presiding officer at the Town Hall.

Outside, many waited anxiously. Mr Rowland continues,

> Messengers were sent to bring in the dilatory and the sluggard. As closing time approached, John Pugh became fearful of the result, and he asked the waterworks manager, named William Jones, to go with him to the railway station, where a number of travelling drapers, all Scots, and members of St David's Church, were due to return home from business. Pugh stood on the one platform and William Jones on the

other. Between them they gathered eight bonnie Scots and marched them to the Town Hall, where they duly recorded their votes. When the result of the poll was declared the next day, there was a majority of eight for the Free Library. So as the result of Pugh's convictions and exertions, Pontypridd had and still has, a splendid Public Library.

In 1884 John's home was the venue for a significant meeting with another minister. They talked together of the needs of the churches which ministered to the people in the English language. John knew that the subject was vital to the future of faith in South Wales. Everything in his background, his up-bringing, his church denomination, the language of his heart, was Welsh. Yet a huge number of the people, and a growing number who were now to be found in places of worship, were able to speak no Welsh. Though the denomination was making no official move to set up an English-speaking network, John was always willing to meet an obvious need himself. At 2:30 in the afternoon of May 8th, 1884, four ministers and nine lay leaders met at John's church in Pontypridd. As well as the subject of the language, they discussed 'the mode of conducting public services and how to meet the young people and win them for the Saviour'.

This area of tension is usually present when a church wakes up and begins to respond to the call to evangelism. A conference was planned to meet in Swansea later that year, followed by a second in Pontypridd in 1885. Edward Davies, the son of David Davies, Llandinam, was willing to be the president. His encouragement, energy, and resources were always available to John. Their closeness was hugely important for what later become known as the Forward Movement. In 1889, a national conference was chaired by Principal Thomas Charles Edwards.

This conference was to serve a number of purposes in the years to come. Significant Christian leaders were invited to bring insights from elsewhere, and they included such famous teachers as F.B. Meyer, P.T. Forsyth and Cambell Morgan.

The conference continued into the 1930s, but by then it's theological emphasis had moved from its beginnings in biblical truth towards liberalism, in which man's mind is seen as equally important as revelation. John's drive in setting up the conference in more orthodox days has tended to be forgotten.

6

To the Great City

The heart of John's work would always be evangelism. He now felt the time had come to move from Pontypridd to a new place for his evangelistic work under the Lord. He is now forty three years of age, and the principles of Gospel Ministry have been well learned.

Work with the Lord is always an adventure, but never a mere human venture. John had to be sure of guidance before the next phase. The principles and methods would always be the same, for they expressed his heart-felt discipleship and determination to be faithful to the vision he'd been given. But the new sphere of work would be even more demanding, a challenge which remained with him to the end of his earthly life. His experiences had provided him with the knowledge and confidence for work in the growing city of Cardiff, which was eventually to become the capital of Wales. He had been led into a rich variety of training for this work, assisting his father in building bridges, with planning, finance, surveying, and man management, and this helped greatly in the building work to come. His experiences of the Lord at work in Tredegar and Pontypridd gave him the utmost confidence in the same blessings in future ministry.

There was a huge need in Cardiff, and a call came to him from leaders of Clifton Street Church. He knew that such a place had much to learn about evangelism. Truly his present work in Pontypridd was far ahead of what he would find there. Another call had come at the same time in 1888 from Glasgow, where his great friend William Ross would have been near. But John was confident that the call to Clifton Street in Newport Road was to provide his next base for work. It was in its early years, after being launched as an English branch of Bethania Welsh Church, in the Docks. John was inducted as minister in January 1889. Though a young church, it was carrying on its activities along the usual traditional lines.

The population of Cardiff was growing very fast, and the churches did not know how to keep in touch with the many. New streets were being built, and people continued to flock in. John understood the great need, and knew he could play a part in meeting it. His daughter writes, 'He saw the great door opening in front of him.'

When he had agreed to come to Clifton Street, the preaching and teaching was done by Dr Cynddylan Jones. He was a well known author, biblical commentator, and speaker, who championed the well-tried orthodox and evangelical teaching. He was widely loved and appreciated in his own and other denominations. Later, in the movement of 1904–1905, he helped by providing a sound historical background for the events taking place. When John came to Cardiff, Dr. Jones was ministering at Clifton Street at least once each month, but there was only a small congregation there to hear the great preacher. John said to him, 'You shall nurture the saints, and I will go after the sinners.'

The revolution started on the Sunday night in Clifton Street, when John delivered his first sermon there. At this time the

'Methodist zeal' of previous generations had almost died. 'When the power to restore the lost has languished in the church, it then ceases to be a church', says John's daughter. The gathering of people can remain a pleasant and comfortable spot in some lives, but without the touch of the Lord it has no future. 'For many years', said one of the Clifton Street deacons, 'I have been dissatisfied because of the absence of a sign of God's power in our meetings.' With the expectation and believing prayer which John exercised on that first Sunday came a new beginning.

The congregation were seeing something unknown to them when those who were moved by the Lord came to the front. The Holy Spirit moved amongst the congregation. It was not contrived or full of noise, but deep, thoughtful and quiet. Sometimes we have experienced moments like this when a large crowd is awed by the reality and closeness of the Lord, and the silence is deep and powerful. John's daughter writes,

> When those who were present spoke of that night, they lowered their voices. God had spoken to them. How, and from where they did not know.

When the Holy Spirit moves in this way it is surprising and unexpected, though we would say we had prayed for His Presence.

At the end of the meeting John asked the congregation to follow him to the school house to hold a prayer meeting. As it progressed, one after another went forward, until there were twenty-two people kneeling in repentance before the Lord.

Early in John's ministry in Clifton Street he came into contact with a young pastor, Revd. F.C. Spurr, of the Baptist Church in Longcross Street, and together they planned an outreach mission. They wanted a united front, and invited the other evangelical ministers to work with them. Many wanted to join this initiative, which gave John real encouragement and delight. It came to be known as the 'Roath United Mission'. The neighbourhood was divided into thirty or forty areas, and each had a chosen helper, who called at every house to inform the folk and invite them to come. A programme was prepared, and in addition to personal contact, which is always the best way of reaching people, posters advertising the evening were placed at strategic places. There were three ingredients in each day, beginning with a prayer time at 7 am and then in the afternoon at 3 pm Bible teaching was provided for anyone who could come. The evenings, at 7:30, were evangelistic in a more explicit way. The result was wonderful. Hundreds yielded to the Lord Jesus and decided to become disciples. Others were touched by the Holy Spirit in many ways, and backsliders reclaimed. In the three months of the mission many were to join the churches of the area. They came in with zeal, hope and enthusiasm, knowing that they had been placed there with a purpose. The composition of those that were converted was striking. Class played a large part in the Victorian society we are encountering. John's daughter writes, 'People of every class in Cardiff gave themselves to Christ'.

John was always looking beyond the walls of his own church building, and even his neighbourhood. He realised how easy it was for his people to be comfortable in their religious behaviour. He saw the area called Splott nearby, with its teeming population, and very few opportunities for the people to be introduced to the love of Father and the person of the Saviour. As he gazed in all directions, he saw the city, with a population of 128,000, mostly outside Christian teaching and witness. If every seat in every meeting place and worship building in Cardiff were filled, there would be no seat for 80,000 people. John knew from experience in Cardiff and previously, that most of the people were unconcerned about their spiritual state. Whatever he could do personally and with close friends, he knew that in addition, there must be an awakening in the established church buildings, English and Welsh speaking, across the city. They must accept their responsibility for the neglected masses. A much larger vision was born in John's heart, nothing less than the whole city of Cardiff for Christ.

One morning in June 1890 John was passing the gate of Cardiff prison. He was always open to 'divine appointments' and as he moved from day to day in his work, he sought guidance for fresh vision. On that day he noticed a crowd waiting outside for the release of some of the prisoners. The crowd would include family members, old friends, no doubt some who had already made plans for further crime. For those who emerged, some would be easily recruited. John watched and saw what was happening. He realised there was no Christian there to show care and concern or to help them with a better future. He walked on, deeply troubled, and decided to write a letter about the situation. He invited others with a similar concern to join him in a ministry to ex-prisoners.

Two well-known industrialists, the brothers John and Richard Cory, who were outspoken Christian men, responded to his letter. They met together and undertook to be president and treasurer of whatever was to be established. Together they visited Major Howard, who had charge of the prison, and talked over the need and the ways in which they would wish to meet it. It was usual for prisoners to be released at 8 am each morning, and from friends of the Cory family and the churches, volunteers were chosen for the work of meeting the released men and women. A breakfast had been provided at the Heathfield Coffee Tavern in South Luton Place, and the invitations were issued. During the morning hymns were sung, and later a message from the Word was shared. It usually contained an invitation to know and follow Jesus, and begin, with help, a new life with Him. By mid 1891 over 2,000 people had responded by coming to the breakfast, and some wonderful conversions had taken place. It was decided to call the work, 'The Society for the Aid of Released Prisoners'.

In that same year the American evangelists, Moody and Sankey visited Cardiff for a mission. Dwight Moody, converted in Boston, had begun a Sunday school in the slums of Chicago in 1858, which, in five years became a church. He was a servant of the YMCA organising teaching conventions for leaders of Sunday schools. He first visited England in 1867, and there was a preaching tour of Britain in 1875, accompanied by Ira Sankey. Their personal meeting had been at a YMCA convention. Together they published 'Sacred Songs', with a great response from churches, for over thirty years. The popular style of these songs became the model for evangelistic song books for a hundred years. All the finance gained by the sales of the song books was given to the trustees of a school Moody had established. Two seminaries were founded in the USA, and when the two evangelists again toured Britain in 1881–1884, they spoke in the universities. The Moody Bible Institute was to be established in 1889 in Chicago.

The 1891 Cardiff venue for the American evangelists was the Wood Street Congregational Church, with seating for up to 2,000. Queues formed from early morning, including many non churchgoers. John Pugh had used the Sankey hymns from his Tredegar days. Church leaders criticised the content for being simplistic and 'lightweight', but John saw this as pride. The superior attitude of leaders made a barrier for ordinary people.

John wanted his daughter to hear and remember the message of Dwight Moody, and they went together to several gatherings.

Then they were invited to the home of Richard Cory where Moody was staying. She wrote,

> Before leaving, my father asked Moody to pray. He later said to me 'This is a good man and one day you'll be glad to know that you met him. I didn't want him to leave Cardiff without you two knowing each other'. Mr Moody invited my father to join him and Sanky in their work in Chicago.

Part of John's answer was that he was called to Cardiff, which was the Chicago of Wales.

Burn Out, Don't Rust

7

Cardiff and Wales for Christ

The growing city was a melting pot, into which people kept pouring, and the majority spoke no Welsh and had little Christian experience. John has usually been credited as the builder of many buildings for Christian use. This is true, and for decades, even a century, they were regarded as a fitting memorial to the originator of what was later named the Forward Movement.

However, John was first of all an evangelist, and a man of the people. Though full of grace towards the great in Society, and an able organiser, he was most at home in the open air or in a tent. In these very visible locations there were far fewer obstacles to the ordinary folk hearing the Good News. There were always negatives in putting resources into magnificent church buildings. R. Tudur Jones, in his detailed analysis of the state of the Christian churches at this time, makes the point powerfully that pride in buildings, architecture, and 'success' brings rivalry and decline. John knew that in the climate of South Wales some covering from the rain, wind, cold and snow was necessary, but the buildings must always be secondary to the message and the presence of the Holy Spirit. Even though walls were necessary, they were a hindrance to those outside. John was ready to organise, but with reservations.

As well as the Cory family, he could also rely upon the Davies family at Llandinam. David Davies had touched his life at an early time in Pembrokshire, and now he could enlist a kindred spirit in Edward Davies, the son. John always felt that the denomination was moving too slowly in evangelism, and after much prayer and planning, a tent was set up in the nearby area of Splott, a teeming working class district. He had learned a great deal from the work of William Ross in Glasgow.

His opponents viewed the project with scorn. One critic declared, 'You might as well try to demolish the rock of Gibraltar with boiled peas as to convert the people of Splott in a tent!' John knew that the battle was the Lord's, not his, and that appearances were superficial. At just this time, guided by the Holy Spirit, Seth Joshua had come to him from Neath, and offered his assistance. Seth and his brother Frank had the same passion as John since their work for Jesus began after conversion about nine years earlier. Their pioneering and compassionate proclamation in an industrial area where the English language was the norm, was a kind of pattern which the Lord was to develop with John. The Joshua brothers had no theological credentials. These two men were truly used in the Neath area, succeeding, as Geraint Fielder says, 'among the down and outs of the unemployed, and the immigrant English labourers who had lost their own roots.'

As John set out on the conquest of Cardiff, he wrote to Edward Davies. He tells us,

> When the deplorable spiritual condition of tens and thousands in Cardiff were almost crushing me, I poured out my soul in a letter to Mr Edward Davies of Llandinam in 1891, asking him to be treasurer to the enterprise before there was a church or a committee at my back.

John was delighted when Edward agreed. Getting him on board meant everything to John. Though the denomination was now seriously looking at the needs of English speakers in the communities, John feared that resolutions would only end in a talking shop and not a transfer to action. In that year a conference had met at Clifton Street, and again for a while there was inertia, neither encouragement nor clear opposition.

So, together John and Seth Joshua set about putting up the tent, borrowed for the purpose of evangelism. The sight of these two big men at work caused interest in the locals. One of the rougher characters of Splott paused to ask Seth what was going on.

'Hello govnor', he asked, 'What's this, a boxing show?'

'There's going to be some boxing here', Seth replied.

'When are you going to start?'

'Tomorrow morning at 11 am.'

'Tomorrow's Sunday.'

'Well, the better the day, the better the deed.'

'Who's on?'

'I've got to take the first round.'

'Who's with you?'

'He's a chap called Beelzebub.'

'Never heard of him, who's he?'

'Oh, he's a smart one I can tell you. Come tomorrow morning.'

'I'll be there'.

On the day, Seth Joshua took the morning and evening services, for John had to fill the two slots at Clifton Street, but he spoke in the afternoon. The man who had spoken to Seth was there, although he must have realised that this was a Christian meeting. The Holy Spirit began to work on his heart and he was converted that day.

From May 5th 1881 until October 13th, when the tent was destroyed by high winds, on Sundays, and on some week days, the Lord worked wonderfully under the canvas, and hundreds were converted. The tent was 30 yards long and eleven yards wide, the earthen floor covered with sawdust. The furniture, seats and platform were simple planks.

John had made no allowance for children. On the first day the tent was to be used, scores of children naturally made their way there. They wanted to see what was happening and to get inside it – it was a real adventure. But there was no room for both adults and children. The next Sunday a larger crowd of children gathered. When John talked with them he made it clear that if there was space, he would want them with him. 'Can't we have a tent Sir?' they asked. He promised them one by the next Sunday. The children went away sure that John would keep his promise. He did, and the next Sunday another tent was placed on the opposite side of the street. In that week the Lord also answered prayer when W.D.O. Jones from Tregarron, was found. He worked in David Page Morgan's shop and was just the man for the children's work. He was willing to come and work with the children in the tent. Pugh wrote later,

> We wonder how we could have been so blind, and how the churches so slow, to see the vital importance of having children saved before they are hardened and marred by sin. In this way did God use the waifs and strays of East Moors to commence a new era in work amongst the children.

To replace the wrecked main tent, by November a large wooden building was put up. It could seat about 500 and was popularly called 'Noah's Ark'. This was followed by a more permanent structure, opened the following Summer – 1892. This could take up to 1,000 people, and became known as East Moors Hall. The wooden building was now used for children and Sunday school work, and even this was replaced a year later by a larger building.

The whole process of the Mission in Splott, or East Moors, had been just what John had hoped. Mr H.G. Howell was to continue the work there, and John and Seth Joshua turned their eyes towards a new area in Canton. While the first tent was still in use, a new tent was erected in that district, and Seth was to be the pioneer. In the following winter, as that tent proved to be inadequate, the gathering moved into the loft over a workshop owned by Mr Marsh, an undertaker. It was affectionately called 'The Upper Room', and was officially recognised as a congregation by the denomination, as was Seth as an evangelist and pastor. By 1894 that work had so grown that a large new building, called the Davies Memorial Hall, in memory of David Davies, was opened, able to seat 1,250. When the work moved from Noah's Ark in East Moors to the new hall, one elderly lady prayed,

> Lord, thank you for this fine building, but we have a
> hiraeth for Noah's Ark. That's where we saw your glory
> and where we first proved the joy of your Salvation.

This mission, progressing through 1891, was soon to be recognised by the denomination and later came to be described as the Forward Movement. John knew that the weakness was the shortage of men who were true evangelists. There was a lack of men gifted enough at getting close to, and through to, the uneducated poor. His doubts about men trained for the ministry of the Presbyterian Church led him to look further afield for the Lord's provision of men. Such a one was H.G. Howell. Under his ministry at East Moors, and later at Monthermer Road Hall, many hundreds were brought to Jesus.

Building on what he had seen in the work in Glasgow, John had evolved the pattern for his evangelistic work in Cardiff. He described it like this:

1. Preaching in the open air, and mission tents all the year round. For the enemy is at work always. He never closes down.

2. If successful, a simple wooden structure to go up next.

3. In due course, bright large halls, are to be built with wide doors and no steps, so that invalid chairs may be wheeled in easily. I see in this point a duel reason. First, the good news is for all. Severe handicap, physical or mental, should not exclude anyone.

   Second, the possibility of Jesus healing work should always be present. Salvation includes not only a new life spiritually, but sometimes the transformation of existence today.

4. To secure men with 'grace, grit and gumption'. The method of work is only useful if the real work of powerful evangelism is enshrined in the men, always guided by the Holy Spirit.

Such men were Seth Joshua and H.G. Howells, and there were many to follow, but never enough.

8

The Forward Movement and 'The Torch'

The work in Canton was next on the agenda of John and Seth. It was well known for its drinking clubs and vice. Previously a non-denominational evangelical group had erected a hall, which could seat 350 in Clive Road. There they met with little blessing, and in September 1891, the sale of the hall was proposed to John, who accepted it at once. Later it was recognised by the denomination.

Mr and Mrs J.E. Ray were asked to lead the Mission there. Johnny Ray was born in Merthyr Tydfil, and was converted in the Rhondda where he had gone looking for employment. He was sixteen at that time, and soon began to preach from the company shop in his Treforest works. He became used to threats on account of his message. Many significant evangelists were saved under his ministry. John wrote,

> The Joshua brothers were brought to decide for Christ through the instrumentality of this humble lad from the Rhondda Valley.

And again,

He has been blessed to hundreds all over the land and
we were glad to have him join heart and hand with our
efforts to win in Cardiff.

One of those converted through his ministry was a Miss Jones,
who gave herself to work amongst women. They later married,
and they worked together in evangelism in Cardiff. They had
already learned many of the lessons of outreach and had grown
'new congregations'. John described the tough situation,

There were two notorious streets on both sides of the
Mission Hall, and the vicinity seemed left without let or
hindrance as the 'happy hunting ground of the enemy'.

The work of the Rays prospered and the fellowship grew with many
new converts. Soon the Hall was inadequate, and was replaced by
larger premises, with the main room seating over 500. The care
for the whole person was emphasized, so the love of Jesus was
demonstrated by word and deed. Great efforts were made in that
area, with many poor broken people, to feed and clothe those
with little to wear. At the time there was great physical hardship
in the Clive Road district, with periodic unemployment for many
men with families. Between 200 and 300 were fed daily in the
hall. By the time that Clive Road Mission was established, the
evangelistic work of John, Seth and the others was being given
the name of the Forward Movement.

The newly recognised movement with its great work of
evangelism in Cardiff, now launched a monthly magazine, which
later became know as 'The Torch'. It had four aims:

1. To encourage others to do what he and his friends
   were doing. An early article was by William Ross. He
   told how the premises at Cowcaddens were available
   to folk round the clock.

2. To follow up the personal decision to follow Jesus, with necessary biblical teaching.

3. To stand against advancing ritualism in the established Church of England and Wales.

4. To let people know of the heritage in which they stood. There was a thrilling history of revival and evangelism in Wales. The magazine included biographies of great Welsh figures of past and present. The most popular feature each month was Seth Joshua's account of missions.

At one time John wondered whether he should continue the work under the Calvinistic Methodist Church or strike out on another line. But he decided to make the movement a spear-head of his own denomination. He felt he was going out like Daniel Rowland and Howell Harris to take the good news of Jesus to the people. He was seeking to be a true Methodist. Within a year, this 'movement' of front line evangelism had been securely established, though not yet given official recognition by the denomination. There were now six mission bases, a membership of 433 believing Christians, 2,680 'hearers' who attended, and a Sunday school work of 1,161.

Through the passion of one minister, John Pugh, with a sense of the desperate need of large areas of Cardiff, things began to change, as he cut through the behaviour of usual church life. He made an appeal to the General Assembly of the Calvinistic Methodists in Liverpool in May 1890, and his old friend, Principal Thomas Charles Edwards, was chosen to Chair a committee to examine the work, which it termed 'New and Strange'! By 1892, the work, now called the Forward Movement was formally taken over by the denomination, and John was recognised as a 'Special

Missioner to give his whole time to the work of the Society'. This was in Machynlleth in June. He now had a committee of godly and forward-looking men to stand with him.

News of the launch of the Forward Movement was shared in every fellowship in the denomination on the first Sunday of 1893, and John hoped that funds would flow to enable an increase in evangelism, securing the right men, and planting in new areas. Sadly there was a lack of urgency and of sacrificial giving, and from the denomination there was never to be enough support.

John was now released from oversight of a congregation, with all its day-to-day pastoral demands, and could give himself to the widening vision. He hoped that even beyond 'Cardiff for Christ', it might become 'Wales for Christ'. Throughout his life, he would act, trusting the Lord to provide, rather than making sure the money and resources were present first. This is always the act of faith of a follower of Jesus, which may look foolish to the faithless, but which is wonderfully vindicated when souls are saved. John would work with any Christian who shared his theology of rescue in a fallen society. Independents and Baptists and Anglicans, like John Griffiths, the Archdeacon of Llandaff, were his close friends and co-workers, but evangelism is always pressing and in a hurry, so John did not have the time for administering and planning large pan-denominational efforts. He knew that so much time could be wasted in endless talk, and so he pressed on from where he was, hoping to take as many as possible with him from his own denomination, and elsewhere.

John's sensitive spirit was frequently hurt by opposition from so-called Christian sources, and from within his own people. It showed itself in a bigoted attitude about the Welsh language. On one occasion a Welsh Calvinistic church refused the loan of an unused school-room to enable a service to take place in the

English tongue. And there was racial prejudice. It was asked 'Why should we cater for the foreigner?' Another attack came from those who did not want money spent on evangelism, regarding it as an extravagance! Critics could not cope with John's energy and sense of urgency. They wanted all the plans, buildings and finance in place before any work was begun. Faith and Holy Spirit-led initiatives did not figure. John had many battles on the floor of the assembly of his own district presbytery. He won most of them, often first reduced to tears by the hardness of heart of the ministers. He knew and often said that opportunities, if not to be for ever lost, must be quickly snapped up.

There was also criticism that some of the evangelists were not 'sufficiently educated'. John replied,

> We have not a single evangelist under the Forward Movement who has not resigned a more remunerative position in other walks of life in order to come to us to work for the Master.

He personally sustained many of the challenges, but he also had much help and encouragement from others. The best motivation of all was the intensity of his conviction that the Lord had called him for this particular work. Even when he was aware that he had got something wrong, it did not cancel his sense of call to enable and establish evangelism. He knew he was understood and supported by the spiritual leaders on his committee.

As practical and financial challenges came, he had on his side Christian men who were leaders in various industries. They were devout men with an awareness of the desperate needs of people in the South Wales towns. From 1881 to the end of his days, John could turn to his good friend, John Cory. Speaking at a church function in 1898, John Cory said to the gathering,

It is God's divine purpose that in saving you, you should all become the saviours of others.

And he added,

I want to impress upon you that, next to the joy of realising one's own Salvation is that of becoming an instrument in God's hands of leading others to the Saviour. There is no worldly happiness that a man has ever experienced that is equal to this.

Towards the end of Cory's life, an anonymous tribute included this testimony:

The gladness of Mr Cory's soul beams in his face; nothing rejoices his heart more than to hear of the extension of the Kingdom which is righteousness, peace and joy in the Holy Ghost.

His good works were many, including a block of buildings for the YMCA, leadership in local education, a recreational institute for the police, and backing for the new hospital for sailors. To aid the temperance cause the Cory Memorial Hall was built, and in many works his brother Richard joined him. They together cheered the heart of John Pugh as he struggled with finding money for evangelistic projects and church planting.

Edward Davies of Llandinam, the son of David Davies, who is often written about in this story, became the Forward Movement's greatest supporter. He regarded himself as a steward of the wealth he had, for the purposes of the Lord. He shared John's concern for the spiritual condition of the great masses of the people in densely populated areas. His finance and spiritual interest were always behind John. On one occasion he said to John, 'You can go on with your work. When a big deficit faces you, the money is sure to come.' In his study at Llandinam were many letters that he had received attacking the Movement and its leaders. They had no effect on him. Revd. Howell Williams writes,

> His heart burned for the success of the Church of Christ and no news stirred him more profoundly as that of men and women reclaimed from the power of sin.

His passing to his Lord, at the age of forty-five, in January 1898, was a great loss to John personally and to the Movement. The support of the Davies family, with the Cory's, had helped to get the work through many difficulties in the early years.

Three college Principals are significant in John's story. D. Charles Davies, T. Charles Edwards and Owen Prys were the three, and Edwards, who appears elsewhere in this story, was the most able, but he left this life in 1900 at the age of fifty-three.

Prys was president of the Movement for forty years. All three in their teaching of prospective ministers lamented the fact that they were not seeing enough men coming to train who had evangelism in their bones. Prys wrote in 1897,

> Churches have become so abominably respectable that ministers have almost got to believe that anything but the Gospel of Christ was what was required.

There was,

> Much preaching without the atoning blood of the Lamb, the cross itself would be hidden, and the churches, despite their respectability, would die in their sins. The Forward Movement has taught them, to some extent at any rate, that only by preaching the great fundamental truths of Christianity could they ever hope to save men to eternal life.

The work of John and the Movement received support and praise from significant leaders of denominations beyond Wales, from the declining Presbyterian Church of England to the Principal of Central College, Kentucky, who wrote, 'The reality surpasses any religious fiction'.

9

To the Nation

By 1892 invitations came pouring in to John in Cardiff to come and tell the story of the strange enterprise and to conduct evangelistic worship services. John felt the time had come for a nationwide offensive. He wished to issue a wake-up call to the churches. They must evangelize in their own districts, and all of them should be a Forward Movement church, in the sense that its principles should be those of the Movement. There was no desire to become a separate organization. The churches should do the work themselves. He wished to kindle renewed passion in the churches for the lost. In the densely populated areas he wished to see one great Home Mission enterprise.

The plan of campaign seems to have been, first to concentrate on the colleges, then the industrial areas, then the key towns. Early in the Summer of 1892, John visited Bala and Trevecca Colleges, at which he gave a talk to the students on 'Grit, Grace and Gumption'. 'Grit' meant moral stamina. 'Grace' meant abounding in the grace of faith, in mighty hope and love. 'Gumption' meant a large measure of common sense. John encouraged the college students to study the methods of well known contemporary soul winners, such as Spurgeon and Moody. But they must also launch out, and practice the work for themselves. The students were encouraged to join in missions in the summer vacation each year, and many did so. John was also thinking of a Training Settlement. It was to provide accommodation for the trainees, and lectures from John and other evangelists, with the visiting of homes and open-air speaking. There would also be evening services in nearby halls. Sadly the settlement never happened, but the summer vacation training bore much fruit. One well-known minister, looking back to those days said, 'The meetings of greatest blessing to me have been the open-air services', and, 'The time I spent at the centres has been one of the greatest training and spiritual blessings to me.' After John went to be with the Lord, Bala Theological College added a year of practical training to its course. That would have blessed John.

In the 1890s, Glamorganshire had the fastest growing population for Great Britain, measured by county. Monmouthshire was fourth. The area of Glamorganshire that should first be the target of the evangelistic crusade was the densely populated Rhondda Valleys. Here and in the seaport towns, preaching had often been to the converted, with little impact on other 'hearers' in the congregations. Many people were happy in the Welsh language and culture of the chapels, and had a sense of responsibility and belonging. Geriant Fielder has reminded us that an evangelistic preacher should speak to the heart, and will not be satisfied at just delivering the message. There must be a passion for souls in the speaker, and a response in those who hear. This must not be only a moving response in the moment of hearing. There must be fruit, in that the hearers not only respond, but have changed lives. The evangelical, like John, must look for 'signs following' at the moment, and especially in the long term future. In the industrial areas John and other workers won the allegiance of folk, Welsh-speaking and English-speaking, and it was allegiance first to Jesus. He was great at getting close to people where they were, both in the streets and in the pulpit.

Some of his workers anticipated the leaders of the 1904 Revival by walking around the building as they ministered, to be close to the people. John spoke several times on a Sunday, perhaps in different locations, but before he spoke he would often sit in the congregation, and seek the guidance of the Holy Spirit on the needs of those around him. He was seeking both the prophetic word for all, but also the word of knowledge for individuals. He also ministered 'at the front' with the local team alongside him, including the local Missioner and the 'Sister', who was active in family work. At the end there would be an extension to an 'after-meeting'. There would be an invitation 'to stand' for prayer for particular need, and many would be counselled in a quiet room. John knew that the real spiritual need of each one must be met. His messages were passionate, which seemed to make response easy. He was always preaching for a verdict. When the leaders in the after-meeting walked amongst the people, the Sister spoke to the ladies and the men to the men. This rule was also kept in the counselling room. In this method John came to know souls in different Halls, and to be closely united in love and fellowship with the Missioners and lady workers. His colleagues loved to work with him, and he loved to share trust and responsibility with them. One Missioner said 'There was nothing so wonderful as the trust he had in us.' This delegation of responsibility helped others to grow. Sometimes he got it wrong, and was very hurt when his trust was misplaced.

In the Rhondda Valleys the population in the 1890s was over 150,000, and little had been done to bring the good news of Jesus to those who had come in from England and Ireland, and other lands. With the backing of the committee in Cardiff, John decided on an initiative in the Rhonddas. He always wanted to begin where he saw the stiffest opposition. In 1891 a centre was opened in Treorchy, for adult evangelism and children's work. You may be surprised that not much is being said about 'youth work', but in those days in working Wales, rural as well as industrial, childhood was short, and often children were at work at the age of twelve, and fully working at the age of fourteen. John already knew Pontypridd, just South of the Rhondda Valleys, so well, and in 1892 a work was done there in the Graig. The work grew, and a church with real missionary zeal was established. The spiritual growth of many people in the district was accompanied by many improvements in social conditions. Crime fell, and people living there gained a greater sense of well-being.

In Porth, 30,000 people lived within a mile of the centre. Christians moved there to begin a work amongst those who spoke no Welsh. However, some English-speaking churches were later to look back and remember that many of them had been founded due to the encouragement and initiative of Welsh-speaking churches. An example was at Blaenau Festiniog, in the slate district of North Wales where forty quarrymen each gave five pounds to help in the funding of a place for those who spoke only English. But, sadly, opposition to change often came from the Welsh-speaking congregations. After much struggle, John and other evangelists found that the best method was to ignore denominational committees and begin a congregational gathering. John, who was then still at Pontypridd, spoke at the opening of that fellowship, which was Methodist in all but name! John remembered what had happened, and a new initiative in 1892 was begun in Porth, under the leadership of John Thomas. He had been converted under the ministry of the Salvation Army at Ystrad Rhondda, and became a personal evangelist. The Lord then called him to be a full time worker. He suffered severe persecution in his work in English cities and Welsh towns, but in 1892 he was appointed to begin the new work at Porth, with the Forward Movement. He began with six helpers in inadequate premises, but quickly the work grew. Tremendous faith prevailed in the small group, and they hired the Town Hall, with seating for 2,500! Soon it was filled every Sunday evening. The basis of the work was open air proclamation and in bad weather a small hall was used. This hall was taken from them by the influence of enemies, mainly in the liquor trade, so that the evangelists worked on the streets in all weathers, and eventually even the Town Hall was denied them on Sundays. However a new site was found, and a corrugated hall erected that could accommodate seven hundred souls. It was opened in 1894, and was well filled.

In that same year, a work began at Treharris in the Taff Valley. Nearby, to the north, was the great centre for industry and population called Merthyr Tydfil. Seth Joshua wrote:

> This is the hardest problem we have ever found as a Movement – a synagogue of Satan where everything cranky-religious and anti-religious finds soil to root.

It was principal Prys who urged John to do something in Merthyr. John was well aware of the area, from the time of his work at Tredegar, only seven miles away, as well as his time at Pontypridd. Pugh carried Merthyr in his heart for a long time, but every avenue seemed closed. He prayed much for the place, asking the Lord to open a way. One day John realised he should rent the Temperance Hall, right in the centre of the town, and begin work there. Later, in March 1905 Seth began a mission there. There was fierce opposition, often from the liquor trade, but Seth kept going in the large Hall on Sundays, and used a Presbyterian school room on week nights. There was also a Welsh language mission in Penydarran, a district in the east of Merthyr, but that work was failing. It had been established with the sacrificial support of a lady from Rhyl in North Wales, Miss Hannah Jones.

She had asked the Lord to show her the place where she could put her meagre resources, for she was not wealthy. But she was faithful, and it was on her death that things became difficult. The younger people there could use English, and so the fellowship became part of the Movement. In the years towards the end of his earthly life, John saw these causes opening in the English language in the valleys of East Glamorganshire. We have already mentioned Treorchy, Porth, Graig, the Merthyr causes and Treharris, and to these were added Cwm Park, Abercynon, Maesteg, Cilfynydd, Penrhiwceiba and Pontygwaith. Each of these centres had a full-time evangelist. Work had also begun in the nearby valleys in Monmouthshire, across the divide of the Rhymney River.

Before the Movement in its official form was three years old, centres with an evangelist were opened at Cross Keys , Abercarn, Abertillery, Elliotstown in New Tredegar and Ebbw Vale. A little later work began at Blaina, Llanhilleth, Pontypool and Six Bells.

As with John in his Tredegar days, John Harris at Elliotstown in the coal mining area began alone. He proclaimed the Good News of the Gospel on the street corners. The crowds of listeners grew night by night. He was able to hire a hall, and soon there were over 50 committed Christians and a school of 200 children. The building was regularly packed with hearers. At Llanhilleth, as in other towns there was what was called 'The Stop Tap Mission', which drew many, especially during the 1904 Revival. On Saturday nights as the drinkers were leaving hotels and public houses, they were met with a Christian team singing and witnessing. Many with a drink problem were transformed as they gave their lives to Jesus.

10

Seaports and 'The Van'

We must now return to the seaport towns of South Wales. They all had a very mixed population, and in Cardiff alone it was estimated that there would be found over 2000 Seamen every day. John wrote that 'Many foreign and British Seamen have met with Salvation in our halls and tents'. The large town and port of Newport in Monmouthshire became a target for John and the Movement in 1895. It had a population of 60,000 and it is estimated that only 8000 people had any connection with a place of worship. Unlike Cardiff and Barry, Newport had long been an important set of docks at the mouth of the River Usk, and a town of consequence. It is recounted that John Wesley, on visiting Newport, declared its people more ignorant of the things of the Lord than the Cherokee Indians he had met in North America. Howell Harris had a rough time on a visit there also. John was delighted when the suggestion of a Newport Mission came from the denomination, via the General Assembly. In August 1895 the Joshua brothers, Seth and Frank, began by displaying many posters announcing their arrival. They then took the Temperance Hall for the next year, and brought their families and possesions with them. They were encouraged by a welcome in the YMCA Hall, where they were allowed to minister. On the first Sunday morning, knowing no-one at all, they found in the Temperance Hall a crowd of about 300, and by the afternoon it had grown to 500. It was packed again in the evening. Many were saved on that day. Congregations became too large for the Hall, and there were overflow meetings held in the Corn Exchange. Often, more than one 'overflow' had to be cared for. After an hour one crowd left, so that another group could come in. The friendly Ebeneza Welsh Church lent its premises for the week nights, and it was full to overflowing. The members of the Welsh congregation there were greatly blessed and encouraged in evangelism. In those first twelve months, the original hundred converts formed a new church, called the Tredegar Hall, and used the Temperance Hall for overflows. The Sunday school building was used, and there was enough seating in the Tredegar Hall for 1200 on Sunday evenings.

The Corn Exchange was used whenever it was needed. The work grew into the new century and the leaders were always on the look out for larger premises. Lord Tredegar, an Anglican, was a friend of evangelism and the Movement, and he gave, at a very small ground rent, a great site in the main street. The Hall, with other rooms also, could hold 2000 when it was opened in 1906. It was known as The Central Hall, Newport. On the first day, the official opening was performed by Mrs Edward Davies, widow of John's friend. John was the Speaker that day, and in the evening there were three addresses to a crowd of 2,500.

In 1896 a work began at the Marshes, and soon a new Hall was put up. Malpas Road was a new part of the town with no place of worship. In 1897, as a venture of faith, Malpas Hall was opened with, as yet, no congregation. In a few months there were 30 members and a Sunday school of 120. A work began in Corporation Road in 1900, and this was followed by a branch in

Havelock Street on Caerleon Road, and another, now known as Stow Park. By the time John died in 1907, the Movement had achieved great things under the Lord in Newport.

John Pugh made his start in Swansea in Rhyddings Field, St Helens, in August 1892. With Morris Morgan he pitched his tent there, and held daily and Sunday meetings until October, when the tent came down for the winter. Prayer continued in a cottage, and by May, 1893, a room was built. This soon proved too small, and by 1899 a large hall was erected. Soon the denomination asked John if he would take over Hebron, an old church where there was a terrible history of disputes and a lack of Christian spirit. John's first act was to dismantle the church, and expel all the nominal members connected with it! He then re-established it, stipulating total abstinence for all members. A visitor wrote of this area that it was 'one of the blackest spots under the sun'. Evangelist Frank Jackson was put in charge.

Back, near his home in Cardiff, in the heart of the city the Hayes was an open triangular space, with market stalls, an area of movement, activity and work, flourishing, especially on Saturdays. Business continued into the evening. On this area the evangelists, especially Seth Joshua, took their stand. Shouts of the market traders, a barrel organ, and the movement of carts and wheel-barrows could not overcome the message of the Gospel. Soon a crowd would gather, there would be opposition, but with good singing and humour in the speaking, the atmosphere would change. A good number met with the Lord and were transformed in those days at the Hayes. There was also conceived a 'Nomadic' centre. In 1897 a van was purchased, to be called 'The Forward Movement on Wheels'! Two men were given the responsibility for it, and it had enough space for a living area for them as they travelled around Wales. It contained a good quantity of Christian books in both languages, and many Bibles for sale – surely a forerunner of 'Operation Mobilisation' in our day. In the first months it visited the western valleys of Monmouthshire, and then on to the densely populated Rhondda Valleys. The evangelists visited homes, gave out tracts, sold literature, and spoke from the platform of the van in the evenings. Often there was close collaboration with a local chapel. In the first year, something like 71,000 people attended the evening meetings, and over 30,000 professed conversion.

Soon a new building on Port Tennant road was opened. Mr and Mrs Ray spoke at a Mission lasting a week. It was crowded and there were many conversions. Eventually, with Mr W. Meredith as the missioner, another building was erected to seat 700 with a school room for 400. The evangelist Phillip Williams, in 1897, with a group of Port Tennant Christians crossed the rail line to the area called 'The Burrows'. It had no provision for Christian faith. The influence of a Sunday school and evening meetings changed the whole atmosphere of the district. A number of buildings became available in Swansea, which had no significant central hall. John spotted the opportunity, and the Movement bought them for £6,100.

The original cost of these premises had been £14,000! There were several halls including a large hall for 15,000 people. This was called Central Hall, and Seth Joshua moved in to work there, in February 1906. There was a constant stream of blessing.

In 1903 another nearby area had seen the purchase of a theatre in Morriston, capable of holding 1800 people. It was to become a spiritual power in the area. Along the coast to the east, Aberavon had an influx of hundreds of workers from England and Ireland to work at building the new docks and railways. A school hall was built there by the Movement at Sand Fields and opened by John in June 1897. When we consider Neath, we remember the work done there from 1882 by both the Joshua brothers, before Seth moved to Cardiff. With the help of the Anglican Archdeacon, John Griffiths, who often spoke with them in the tent, the work prospered. Seth left to join John in Cardiff, but Frank continued, and in 1902 the Mission was added to the Movement. The result was the need for a large hall, and by August it was opened during a mission led by Seth. In the first six months of its life, over 1000 folk testified to their new life in Jesus.

The creation of Barry Town to the west of Cardiff and the very important docks there was the vision of the great David Davies, who is so much a part of the story of John Pugh. Following the opening up of the huge coalfields of the Rhondda Valleys, Davies was eventually able to export the coal through his newly built Barry Docks, from 1897. Barry became the largest coal-exporting port in the world. It was a rough place with little happening spiritually. 1903 saw the opening of the Dinam Hall, which was the result of Edward Davies concern at the end of his life. The congregation there included sailors from all over the world. There was also a work on Barry Island.

John's excursions took a heavy toll on his health. In 1896 he went for a change of climate to South Africa, where he was able to speak to Welsh settlers in their native language. John was accompanied by Revd. William Lewis. They were shocked by the conditions prevailing in the towns, especially Johannesburg. The Presbyterian churches there had great needs, and on his return, John set about making this known.

John and his family left Clifton Street and moved to Grangetown. He had an eye open always for a site in a needy area, and he soon found one, in May 1893. The site was given by Mr Samuel Mildon. Again, there was a tent Mission, then a 'Tin Church'. A new large hall was opened in 1895, when one of the three addresses was given by Mr William Abraham – 'Mabon'. Having begun in Grangetown, John now looked to the neighbouring district of Saltmead, a very wild place. There were rows of over-crowded houses, and streets inhabited by prostitutes. He and Richard Burgess took possession of a piece of vacant ground and started clearing away the stones and rubbish so that the tent could go up. Stones were now thrown at the tent as the gatherings took place. Again a small hall was needed, which was later replaced by a large hall!

For seven years the Cardiff committee of the Movement had asked for a work to begin in Cathays. Finally an excellent site was found in the area called Crwys, with no single place of worship. John wished to have large halls in significant places, and so in sheer faith two rooms were hired to begin the mission while work went ahead on building a large hall. The first room, in Dalcross Street, could take 300 people. The second was nearby in Fitzroy Street, a room that had previously been a drinking club. It was stated at the time:

> If a man wants to know the rough side of the Forward Movement Mission, let him go to Fitzroy Street for three months.

As this work progressed, the expensive site on Monthermer Road was being developed into Crwys Hall. A third of the large cost was borne by Charles Peirce of Bangor, and so the lecture hall built with the Crwys Hall was named 'The Pierce Memorial Hall'. Early in 1900 there was a formal opening. Memorial stones were laid, and those who took part form a roll of honour for the Forward Movement. John's passion and supernatural strength for gathering in the lost was backed by many who gave all they had to bring about this great story of loving and deeply caring evangelism. Richard Cory's daughter laid one stone, after the first was laid in memory of Edward Davies of Llandinam. Mrs Pugh laid one representing the Sunday school work. She said,

> This fine building will be no Sanctuary unless it is always regarded as the home of the people. Here the outcast and the fallen should be able to come to the Father's arms.

She also gave a philosophy from the heart of the Movement:

> To bring sin-stricken men and women to a Saviour who can take their burdens away, to sweeten lives made bitter by the disappointments of life, to keep children from the darkest and saddest side of life.

Later the Sunday school was to exceed a thousand children.

11

The Women's Work

While John was away in the United States in 1900, a group of ladies had been meeting with his wife, and on his return they appealed to him to start a work of salvation for the neglected people and children of the Heath district, separated from the Cathays site by a large cemetery, together with the usual open-air work, tent missions and work in the small hall. A large hall on Whitchurch Road was built by 1906, which could seat 900 people.

In 1899 John was invited as a delegate to the Pan-Presbyterian Alliance in Washington, USA. The challenging approach of the evangelist shook the staid Presbyterians as he told the story of his work. He even managed to get them to sing with him a favourite hymn from Moody and Sankey, not at all what they would normally do. John was quoted in *The Washington Post*, and later expressed his observations on the Assembly. He said that it lacked enthusiasm: 'There was not sufficient Methodism in it'. John spoke in Welsh churches, and even met the US President, McKinley. Before he left the States for home, the University of Kentucky conferred upon him the honorary degree of Doctor of Divinity, though he only found out that news when back in Wales!

The Pughs were very aware of the many poor girls, often only children, who drifted to Cardiff, and 'lived rough'. There was a silence in polite society in Wales about the sexual exploitation of these girls. The churches did not take any notice of the situation. In England, evangelical societies had broken through this barrier. John's approach was inspired by his friend, Revd. William Ross in Glasgow. In 1893, John took his daughter, then nineteen, to the Cowcaddens Convention. She went out with one of the 'Sisters of the People', into the crowded Streets of Glasgow. The Sisters were made up of Christian nurses who worked with the poorest people and Sisters who had been taught at Sauchiehall Street Bible Institute, and went out at night to contact the prostitutes. These wonderful women lived amongst the needy ones of the city. The work produced an overall decline in crime and violence in the area, and many came to faith in Jesus. Dressed as a Sister, Ann Pugh talked with and gave a flower to a girl in a doorway looking for customers. The girl said, 'It's been a long time since a respectable girl even spoke to me at all'. They invited the girl to come to the Sister's home room. She came that same evening, saying, 'I want you to help me'. Back in Cardiff in 1894 the Women's Branch of the Forward Movement began. Sargent Barker, the evangelist at Saltmead Hall described the situation there, just like Glasgow: 'These girls are expected to adopt this life even by some of their parents'.

Mrs Pugh was the driving force in this compassionate outreach. John said that no-one could really evangelise the cities like Cardiff without,

> Christ-posessed women to go in and out among the suffering poor. There is a work that no-one can do for Christ but them.

And so were appointed 'Sisters of the People', and fine women volunteered to work out of many centres. By 1905 a home was established in two houses in Grangetown, named Treborth Home. Here girls who had left the streets were treated well and helped to find alternative work, and children were looked after so that their mothers could go to work. In the first years the home cared for one hundred and twenty-six women, girls, and babies. The home grew, and moved to a large house in Canton. The Sisters could go where men could not, and therefore reach the women individually. The Lord blessed this ministry greatly, with hundreds led to Christ, lives that were mended, and a new life begun for many. Mrs Tydfil Thomas in 1903 became organiser of the Women's Section.

12

Other Preparations For Revival

In the well documented Revival of 1904–1905, people involved would have heard of the movement of the Holy Spirit in 1858–1863 in America, in Great Britain, especially in Ulster and many other places. Scandinavia, where a quarter of a million people were converted in twelve months. Australia and India were powerfully changed. Also the existing missionary societies in Britain were renewed and challenged, and new missions, like the China Inland Mission, begun. But they might also have been aware of revivals in Wales between 1858 and 1904.

This story, of the person and work of John Pugh, must stand with the many events of revival in Wales during his ministry. John wanted to stand alongside and encourage all of them. The people of Abermeurig, Cardiganshire, maintained a prayer meeting until 1904. Of particular preparation for John, were the events from 1866 in Tredegar. A group of English-speaking Wesleyans and Congregationalists were praying together. A cholera epidemic caused great fear in the town, and people were given a stark awareness of the issues of life and death, never far from the consciousness of people in that tough industrial environment. But with natural fear, came also an opening to the Spirit of the Lord. The revival spread to other church gatherings in town, both Welsh- and English-speaking. Numbers of young people were converted, but also many 'hearers' who had been attending churches for years, but had made no previous beginning of a new life with Jesus. Revival hymns became widely used, like *My Jesus, I love Thee, I know Thou art mine.* Sometimes conviction did not lead fully on to conversion, and probably some were received into membership too soon. A lesson for all time is that care must be taken of new converts.

At the same time as these events in Tredegar, Aberavon experienced an awakening, based on prayer in the churches, and this became the talk of people throughout the community. In 1871, Lord Radstock spoke to a large crowd in the Drill Hall in Newport. A small group had been praying each week. A large number came forward as 'seekers' at the end of the evening. In Cardiff at the same time, Robert Aitken was the evangelist. Over about six weeks in these two missions, 600 people came forward for spiritual help. There were reports of similar renewal in parts of the Rhondda Valleys, but it was in the years 1876–1879 that the Rhonddas experienced awakening. In the first year General Booth of the Salvation Army visited, and next year there were many conversions at Noddfa in Treorchy, and 106 became Members. In Hebron, Ton Pentre, in one month 70 were admitted into membership. In the 1880s the ministry of Richard Owen came to the fore. From childhood he knew the voice of the Holy Spirit as he read the Word. He often wept in his seat as the Scriptures were opened. He was blessed by the events of 1859, and in 1875 in Liverpool he heard DL Moody, and was impressed by his directness. When evangelising, Richard would encourage enquirers to come to an after-meeting, for prayer. He travelled mainly in North Wales, especially in Anglesey and Caernarvonshire, holding meetings from village to village. People came in hundreds and were touched by the Holy Spirit. When Richard went to his Lord at the age of only forty-eight, it was claimed that under his ministry 13,000 souls had been brought to faith in Jesus.

Articles in *Y Tyst*, a denominational news paper, described a number of revivals at unknown places, but mentioned especially Alltwen, where two hundred and thirty were added in two months. 1887 was a special year. A New Year's Day prayer took place at Penuel, Carmarthen, which was the moment for a touch from the Lord. Meetings continued for nine weeks, with people from many congregations, English and Welsh, attending. In one service alone, eighty people were baptised. There were also moves of the Holy Spirit in Llandeilo, and Bangor. An awakening in Blaenau Ffestiniog was linked to the arrival of the Salvation Army.

In the 1890s there were numerous local revivals in Wales. In Caersalem, in Dowlais, a time was set for prayers each day at 10 o'clock. Even those underground would stop work and pray. The church also held open air services. Thirty-six people were added to the membership, and in 1891 it was ninety-four. The influence of the Lord was felt in every corner of the town. In 1892, in August, great freedom was experienced at a meeting in Pontnewydd. It was agreed to go on meeting daily, and for eight weeks it continued. In September, on one Sunday, one hundred and four people were baptised. In these weeks one hundred and sixty-five people became Members. In Nantyglo there were also moves of the Holy Spirit. In 1898, with the church in Abercannaid, Merthyr Tydfil, at a low ebb, and industrial unrest taking place, one lady encouraged the minister, saying that the dawn was about to break. It did that year. In Merthyr, just up the road, there was refreshing, and in Llandeilo, and also in the village of Llandinam, home of the lovely Davies family.

Despite all these signs of the Lord at work, aggressive evangelism was not common. The Home Missions of the Baptists and Congregationalists were not breaking through in Wales. Yet there were outstanding individual evangelists, like Rosina Davies of the Calvinistic Methodists, and Hugh Hughes and John Evans of the Weslyans. Rosina had been saved under the ministry of the Salvation Army. Their work kept alive the memories of 1859, and created a desire for revival. Under Rosina and Betsan Nicholas, life came again to Tai Bach, Port Talbot. Rosina would add to the traditional order of worship a time of openness with prayers and hymns of the Sankey type. After the word, those seeking salvation were asked to remain seated. As Rosina spoke with them, she would send them to seats available at the front, where she could address them. The attitude towards a woman evangelist like Rosina, and women in general, was changing. Sarah Jane Rees and Mrs Penn-Lewis were champions of women in ministry. Mother (Kate) Shepherd's work in the Rhonddas and Aberdare also won much support for this move.

After the first 'Keswick in Wales' Convention in 1903, the Forward Movement's Women's Branch was formed. And so, as John laboured in evangelism, many had been prepared for a nationwide revival. John knew that his work had been a preparation. He said, in 1904,

> It prepared for the present gracious revival which is such a blessing.

His work called the church to see and meet the great needs in South Wales, and as he said,

> . . . urging upon people, by precept and example, to seek the Baptism of the Holy Ghost for Christian Service and Soul Winning.

While Revival is always, when genuine, a sovereign act of the Holy Spirit, we can usually discern, perhaps for a long period, a work of preparation. This too, is a work of the Holy Spirit, as He gives the souls of Jesus' disciples a longing that He might be magnified. There is a longing, a crying out, a seriousness in prayer, and a growing passion for the lost. This preparation is present in Wales, in the life of John and others, in the years leading up to 1904. We must see, as John did, that the Church has lost it's way if it does not trust the leadership of the Holy Spirit, and if it does not have a passionate concern for the lost – a 'love, vast as the ocean'. The anointing on Evan Roberts did not begin, either, at Blaenanerch, for it was upon him in months of intercession at home. He even had a prophetic vision of what was to come in Wales. But it was on that day, on the Cardiganshire coast, that he felt the longing more deeply, and something came to birth. In the prayer meeting Seth Joshua prayed, and the prayer was also the burden on Evan's heart.

With all that followed that year and the next, a tide of reviving power swept in. The halls in many places, built in faith, with no little difficulty, would fill not with comfortable Christians, but with earnest praying folk, urgent in the need to see loved ones, family and friends, saved. Whatever the critics might say, and there was something of the flesh present, what we see is a harvest for Jesus.

13

Revival and John's Departure

John took only a small part in those exciting years. The fact is that he was worn out and almost at the end of his earthly service. He had been the great strong man, fighting in every way and every day for the primacy of evangelism. In the many-sided tasks as Superintendent of the Forward Movement he had to attend to duties which would not be his first choice. In fact he was well-suited for them all. The Lord had prepared him over his lifetime for the planning, building, and financial chores. And he often had to wrestle with committees and other leaders to reach the vision. For years it had taken its toll. It was his faithful friend and co-worker, Seth Joshua, who was more used in the Revival. A new impetus and power seized Seth during those times as he travelled all over Wales.

In December, the full tide of the Holy Spirit flowed in Cardiff. As the anointing fell on hundreds in the church services, they poured out into the open air singing and praying and praising. The people spoke freely to passers by. There was an open hostility in some congregations, but many began to be converted. John saw in the events of the Revival something that gladdened his heart. As in his own ministry on the streets, there was a challenge to the often intellectual, but dead, spirit that prevailed. Men, in their college days had come to covet the role and life-style of the minister, with its securities and honours. Some had become engrossed in wonderfully constructed sermons, and poetic delivery. Their faith was weakened by humanist tendencies and liberal attacks. The whole purpose of their life was lost in cultural persuits. John, in delighting in the moves of the Holy Spirit, knew that those responding in revival days also sometimes carried the flesh into their responses. The emotional excitement could lead to a superficial response, and conversions that were not really conversions at all, which would not stand the test of time.

The Forward Movement Halls were blessed, and became afresh the foundation for a new period of outreach. *The Torch* reported on the Heath Hall:

> Our Heath Centre is all alive with revival fire, and the hall has become too small . . . to receive all the people who are anxious hear the word of life.

As a result of the revival, a new building which could hold 850 people was put up. John himself was there for the laying of the foundation stones on April 4th, 1906. The Pastor there, John Thomas, had been chosen as an assistant to John Pugh in his wider work.

A number of generous benefactors were being called home by the Lord. John Cory was to live until just after John went home to Glory. In early 1906, John and Marie had travelled to the Holy Land, and they saw twentieth-century Jerusalem. In September 1906 he was at the opening of the Pierce Hall, the school room of Crwys Hall. As winter came, John became more tired and ill. He spoke, against his doctors advice, one last time on 'Examine yourselves, whether you be in the faith' 2 Corinthians 13 v 5. After this, he was to be at home with no more journeys. His last public words appeared in *The Torch* of March 1907:

> The Prince of Peace is with us in our attempt to rescue perishing humanity. Must we go back? The cry from Liverpool, London, Bristol and from two dozen densely populated areas in Glamorgan and Monmouthshire for the help of the Forward Movement is heart rending to those who know their spiritual needs.
>
> Are we to retreat owing to lack of funds? Some of the most talented and Spirit-filled ministers have joined our ranks recently.
>
> We need more. With loyal support and the cheer of God's people we won't go back.

Visits from Seth were precious to John, as the two comrade evangelists shared their memories, experiences and hopes. John was sure he would soon be called to meet the Lord he had served with such fervour and energy for so long. He died on Palm Sunday, March 24th, 1907. To the last he was not thinking of himself, but of the people of Wales. His daughter, Annie, tells us of the response to the news of his passing: 'Some wept loudly, others sighed'. Many could not get on with their day's work. A characteristic comment was, 'As soon as the news came I went home: I could not remain where I was'. Annie also informs us of his last moments.

> A short while before he left us I was sitting with him in his room when the Revd F.W. Cole came in. He prayed with us, and when he had finished my father said, 'Francis, will you take charge of Heath Hall? They are without a minister and there is a great opportunity for the Kingdom of God'.

He promised to do so. His doctors believed that if he had not burnt out, he could have had a much longer life. 'But', reports Annie,

> my father said, taking hold of my hand, The Saviour died when He was thirty-three and I am sixty. Don't 'rust'. Wear yourself out for His sake, my child".

Those were his last words.

His coffin was carried on the following Thursday to Crwys Hall, after a short service at the house. It was packed with people many hours before the thanksgiving service began. In the Hall everyone stood, and there spread a wave of triumph and hope and sympathy for others, which supported everyone. It was not like a funeral at all. There were moving words from the Revd Dr J. Morgan Jones, who presided. He showed how, when the churches did little to reach the many lost souls of Wales, John came forward and threw himself into the work. He fired others with his vision, and with the help of Edward Davies and others, he moved many in the churches to act. Then, Revd W. Jenkins spoke of John as a friend throughout his life. Many were attached to him as their Supervisor. John's heart was always open to those in the gutter. So he urged, 'let there be no end to his work'. It was pointed out that John was in the same mould as Daniel Rowland and Howell Harris.

Lord Pontypridd spoke of his limitless faith and unconquerable courage. Let them thank God for such a man, for he fulfilled a great work in the city of Cardiff and throughout Wales.

The real funeral service took place around the grave in Cardiff cemetery, before the procession arrived. There had gathered many hundreds, some of the most poverty-stricken friends from the centres. Many had walked great distances. Annie writes,

> They stood along the edges of the path, as the coffin

was carried to the grave, and the Service was entirely theirs. It was very fitting that they should be the Guard of Honour, and no one else had more right to form it than they had.

Long before that final hour they had been standing and worshipping in well loved hymns and songs. Jack Turner, from Saltmead Hall, shouted loudly,

> Brethren, there is one thing that John Pugh would have liked us to do above all else, that is to give ourselves to Christ. If we have not already done so, let us do it now, and anew, and totally, as he taught us to do, so that we may be worthy of standing by his grave. May this day, friends, be a turning point in our history, and the beginning of a better life.

'Amen!', 'I agree', said so many in response, and wept again, and they were men in the main, not ladies. Revd John Williams, Penygarn, committed the body of John to the ground and said that long after this day John's work would continue to bear fruit. Seth led the final hymn, *Oh fryniau Caersalem*.

14

David Davies – His Contribution

The story of John Pugh could not be told, except for the
background of the story of David Davies of Llandinam. In
fact this is, in reality, not the story of John and Marie, David and
Edward Davies or the Joshua brothers, but the wonderful story
of the Lord, the Holy Spirit, who puts them all together for His
purposes. As in the Acts of the Apostles in the New Testament,
the Lord works at the same period, time, or moment to bring
together those whom He wishes to use.

It is a work of love, so that many others may be helped and
saved. So in any moment in history, the Lord weaves a tapestry,
or creates a network, to reach out to the lost. Many strands work
together in this great purpose. In John Pugh's life, David Davies
is central, touching it at many points and enabling much.

David was older, born in 1818, from the same part of Wales as
John, at Llandinam. From humble beginnings on a small farm,
the eldest of nine children, he was educated in the village school,
but at eleven years of age he began work on the farm. For the
next twenty years he was engaged in hard manual toil. By his
great efforts and his own God-given gifts, he was able to grow
to independence and eventually to great ventures which changed
Wales. In his labouring on the farms, and the development of

his work as a sawyer, he always put first his spiritual health. The family worshipped together and from his early years he became aware of the Lord Jesus as his Saviour, and of the need for divine guidance in his life. He was twenty-seven years of age when his father died, and he took on the responsibility for supporting his mother and the other children. He was good at estimating the value of a piece of work, and making a bargain. While supporting the family he twice moved to improve his land, and was at many auctions looking for good breeding beasts.

The county surveyor, Thomas Penson, first used him on a project for a new bridge over the Severn. David had met the love of his life, Margaret Jones. She was a great girl, a fervent Christian, and they were married in May, 1851. In June 1852, Edward was born. David was now aware of a big opening. The county was eager to develop railways. With a co-worker, he began to build the Llanidloes and Newtown Railway. In 1862 he was invited to Sardinia to advise on railway construction. Then, in that year, he began work on the Pembroke and Tenby Railway, where the relationship with John Pugh Senior continued, and where he came to know our John Pugh.

A great factor of his success in life was the good relations he always maintained with his men. This can be described as part brotherliness, part paternalism. He was one of the men as he worked, with great physical strength and abounding energy. Men wanted to work for him. He joined in on meal times and entertainments. As a Christian example, he cared for their morals and taught thrift and temperance. On the Pembroke and Tenby Railway, David built a large workshop at 'Starvation', an isolated dreary place. He began a Sunday school there, and it was there that John Pugh began to be influenced. Thomas Charles Edwards and others ministered there, and in time John Pugh himself began to preach. Similar provision was made at Narbeth.

David sought to be elected to Parliament, but failed at the first attempt. For a lowlyborn non-conformist to stand for Parliament was considered outrageous in the Wales of 1865. The seats, for a length of time, had been at the disposal of the great landowners. Many ordinary folk were penalised when they failed to vote as the aristocracy dictated. But things were changing. In 1880 only two Tories were returned in Wales, and twenty-eight Liberals, representing the working people. David had played his part in preparing for this.

David's secretary, Webb, had a connection with the developing coal interest, especially in the Rhondda Valleys, and astute folk knew that there were vast coal reserves in the Upper Rhondda. David was contacted and asked if he was interested. He was looking for a new venture for his energy and his capital. He took a lease on minerals on land at Treochy owned by Crawshay Bailey. A parcel of 849 acres was obtained. With two other leases, eventually, David and his friends were able to build up an unbroken property of 8000 acres. Two pits were sunk in 1865, then there was a period of more than a year with no sign of coal. One morning David told his workers that he could not go on, as he was at the end of his money. His men met together and agreed that as David was such a good employer, they would work on for a week with no pay. During that final week one of the finest seams of coal in the world was struck at a depth of 220 yards. Later the lower seam of coal was reached at a depth of 240 yards. His men were liberally rewarded. Not long afterwards, the upper seam was struck at Park at a depth of 140 yards down, and the lower one at 156 yards. Production began, and the coal David had found had no rival in the world. It was excellent for the steam ships of the world's navies. David's company was called 'The Ocean', and he was often to be seen underground, regretting that as the work grew he could not know personally, each of the workers, as he had when developing the railways. Davies worked with others, including the Cory family, in the industrial development of South Wales. The railways and dock companies were unprepared for this huge expansion. There were many log-jams and delays, and David, while not wanting to criticise the transport workers, pointed out in 1873, that the time must soon come for major improvements. But the Taff Vale Railway, and the Bute Docks at Cardiff did not seem to change anything. David and other industrialists, decided to establish a new dock.

They chose a small village, Barry, seven miles to the West of Cardiff, to be connected with the Rhondda by a new railway. In 1885, after a parliamentary battle with the Bute interests, work began at Barry, and by 1889, the dock was in use. Once again aware of the Lord's guidance and blessing, David had achieved something amazing. The town of Barry was built, and the docks there were to overtake those at Cardiff.

Throughout his life, he had put much of his wealth in two areas that really mattered. He always felt that his workers should be properly rewarded, and they were, even though there were lean times in the industries. But above all he wanted to back up the Christian evangelism amongst the people and their families. So John Pugh and his evangelists, and the development of the Forward Movement were to rely on this backing. It was to continue not only in David's lifetime, but also in that of his son. David's power, and his vision, did not decline as he approached old age. With the new dock, went the creation of a whole new community at Barry. He went home to his Lord 1890, having seen so many of his hopes come to fruition.

Bibliography

General

Faith and the Crisis of a Nation by R Tudur Jones
University of Wales Press, Cardiff 2004

Fire on the Altar by Noel Gibbard
Bryntirion Press, 2005. Especially chapter 1

Publications which include information on John Pugh

The Romance of the Forward Movement by Rev Howell Williams
Cardiff, 1946

Atgofion am John Pugh in Welsh, by John Pugh's daughter, Annie
Pugh Williams
Published by Gwasg Gomer, Llandysul

Grace, Grit and Gumption by Geraint Fielder
Published by Christian Focus Publications, 2000